CHINA

PHOTOGRAPHS BY

EVE ARNOLD
BRUNO BARBEY
WALTER BOSSHARD
RENÉ BURRI
ROBERT CAPA
HENRI CARTIER-BRESSON
RAYMOND DEPARDON
ELLIOTT ERWITT
MARTINE FRANCK
HIROSHI HAMAYA
THOMAS HOPKER
HIROJI KUBOTA
GUY LE QUEREC
COSTAS MANOS
INGE MORATH
MARC RIBOUD
HELEN SNOW
PATRICK ZACHMANN

OF MAGNUM

CHINA

A PHOTOHISTORY 1937-1987

INTRODUCTION BY JONATHAN D. SPENCE

EDITED WITH COMMENTARIES BY W.J.F. JENNER

THAMES AND HUDSON

CONTENTS

Introduction by Jonathan D. Spence

URING much of the fifty years of Chinese experience that is caught in these photographs, the country was a prey to terrifying, mind-defying violence. For eight of these years, from 1937 to 1945, the Chinese faced the Japanese in full-scale warfare. For four more years, from 1945 to 1949, the country almost tore itself apart in bitter civil war. From 1950 to 1953 China was caught up in the Korean War. Thereafter, though there were no more major international conflicts, patterns of domestic consolidation were shattered twice by giant upheavals arising from internal ideological disagreements about the correct form of China's Socialist Society. From 1958 to 1962 the accelerated communization process known as the Great Leap Forward led to disruption and death across great swathes of the country; while from 1966 to 1976 the 'Great Proletarian Cultural Revolution' tormented millions more and led to the near total demoralization of the bureaucracy and the intelligentsia.

Yet the patterns of this violence were not random, and the Chinese continued to live in hope, first for national reunification and – after that was largely realized in 1949 – for the transformation of their society and economy. Within each of these sectors of hope, however, were embedded seeds of further conflict. Between 1937 and 1949 Chiang Kai-shek and the Kuomintang or 'Nationalist Party' held out an alternate vision to Mao Zedong's socialist solutions. And from 1956 through into the late 1980s senior leaders of the Chinese Communist Party disagreed profoundly among themselves as to what the correct course for China's societal and economic regeneration should be. The result was a prolonged series of power-struggles inside China, conducted sometimes in secret but also at times in the full glare of national publicity, with the accompanying trappings of a 'mass campaign' and the subsequent humiliation of the vanquished.

Despite the pervasiveness of the camera as a major recorder of our lives in the twentieth century, surprisingly large portions of the Chinese story are still not available in any visual form. And among the pictures that were taken and are currently available to view, a high proportion of the most powerful ones came from photographers in the Magnum international photographers' cooperative. Since Magnum was not founded until 1947, many of

7

the photos in Section II of this volume for the period from 1937 to 1947 are not technically Magnum photographs, and some were shot under contract with other journals or agencies, but the four photographers represented here all had close Magnum contacts. Robert Capa and Henri Cartier-Bresson were among the co-founders of the cooperative, as they sought greater artistic control over their own work, and freedom to print what they chose and to keep their own negatives. Helen Snow and Walter Bosshard, though not formal members of Magnum, were later represented by the cooperative.

THE images from 1937 and 1938 are especially powerful and moving ones. As far as China was concerned, the summer of 1937 marked the beginning of World War II, even if few people at the time realized this. The Japanese provocations of that year, though initially no bolder than a number of parallel blows against China that had occurred in 1928, 1931, 1932 and 1934, came at a time when the Nationalist leader Chiang Kai-shek was facing overwhelming domestic pressure to give up his long struggle with the Chinese Communists, which he had been waging since 1927, and to forge a new government of national unity. At the same time the Communists, driven out of central and eastern China by Chiang, were isolated in northern China and seemed on the verge of extinction as an organized political force. They had little to lose by forging a temporary alliance with Chiang, and much to gain in the form of time to rebuild their fractured forces.

Robert Capa caught this mood well, with his photographs of the Chinese boy scouts marching under their Kuomintang banners with anti-Japanese slogans (26), and of other children studying posters that urge return and reconquest of the Manchurian hinterland (27). Other Capa photos, like his young soldier in a German-style steel helmet (21), remind us of another side of the coin, the fact that the Kuomintang army's training had been supervised, since the early 1930s, by a succession of senior German military officers working under contract for Chiang Kai-shek while Chiang himself had been forging an ideological programme that drew heavily on elements from Italian fascism as well as from China's own traditional Confucian philosophy.

Such an ideology was not likely to coexist easily with Communism, even if Helen Snow's photograph of 1937 seems to symbolize the reality of a United Front, as the three saluting soldiers stand smiling under the crossed flags of the Kuomintang sun and the Soviet hammer and sickle (19). Helen Snow, who wrote powerfully on the radical students' and women's movements of China in the late thirties under the pseudonym of Nym Wales, took this photograph and others of the Chinese Communist units while she was in Yan'an during 1937. The previous year her husband Edgar Snow had visited the Communist base area near Yan'an, and conducted the protracted series of interviews with Mao Zedong and other Communist Party leaders which were subsequently published as the moving and influential book *Red Star over China*. Helen Snow, in her pictures, caught the mood of relaxed yet determined radical commitment that seemed to pervade the Communist forces at this time, a mood that mirrored that which could be found among the loyalist forces in the Spanish Civil War.

But if Yan'an was something of a haven, in China at large the war was proceeding with its ghastly toll of casualties. Chiang Kai-shek, having tried in vain to hold a defensive perimeter against the Japanese in the area inland from Shanghai during the summer and autumn of 1937, was finally forced back in a retreat that turned into a rout, first to Nanjing, and then far up the River Yangzi to Wuhan (an industrial complex of three cities, one of which was Hankou). Here in 1938 he tried to make a new stand against the Japanese, with the remnants of his best troops, aided now – as the United Front briefly remained a reality – by the warplanes and pilots sent to help the Chinese cause by the Soviet Union.

Neither Britain, France nor the United States came to China's aid, and the war continued to go against the Nationalists. One brief moment of Chinese glory came at the great pitched battles of Taierzhuang, in eastern China, where Chinese forces beat back a major Japanese drive. Robert Capa covered this fighting in the spring of 1938, and caught the sense of professional skill and determination in the field that the Chinese ground forces were capable of (37,38). But the Chinese were unable to follow up on their victory, and the melancholy catalogue of wrecked hopes and shattered cities began anew, until Hankou too was abandoned, and Chiang's base established still farther west down the Yangzi, in the Sichuan city of Chongquing (Chungking).

The agonizing years of the long war of attrition with Japan, and the corresponding slide of morale among Kuomintang forces and the growth of the territory controlled by the Communist 'border area governments' and guerrilla forces in the north and the east of China, are not chronicled in this volume. Nor are the early years of civil war between the Nationalists and the Communists, which resumed almost as soon as the Japanese surrendered in August 1945, and continued (with a brief respite during the American general George Marshall's cease-fire mission of 1946) until the final collapse of the Nationalist armies in 1949. But the very last year of the civil war was captured with extraordinary force by one of Magnum's co-founders, Henri Cartier-Bresson. His cycle of photographs from the spring of that year form an essential addition to the historian's record, which can only catch in words the tangled details of Kuomintang military defeat, galloping inflation which resulted in the collapse of the Chinese financial system altogether, and the disillusionment of students and educated Chinese with their government which was to make them – if not pro-Communist – at least the wary welcomers of their new conquerors who chose to speak in their name. Cartier-Bresson's bemused old bearded man in Peking (42), the tired young Communist soldier striding into Nanjing (43), the excited yet disorganized women demonstrators in Shanghai (44), the union members hefting their banner of a youthful-looking Chairman Mao (45), the still dapper yet gaunt and beaten Nationalist officer awaiting evacuation (41), all of these images were central to the story that had been unfolding, and was to continue to unfold after the official declaration of the founding of the People's Republic of China in October 1949.

THERE is no way of knowing what kind of a photographic record might have been made of the early years of the People's Republic had the Korean War not broken out, though the confiscation by the Chinese Communists of all Cartier-Bresson's photographs made in Shandong province early in 1949 show that the task would never have been easy, nor the photographer's presence uncontroversial. In the event, the entry of China into the Korean War late in 1950 led to a phase of intense anti-Westernism in China, manifested through the massive rallies of the 'Resist America Aid Korea' campaigns, the attacks against professional trained managerial and technical personnel (many of whom had worked for, or been trained in, Western businesses), the thought-reform (or 'brain-washing') carried out on certain Westerners or Chinese sympathetic to Western modes, and eventually to the expropriation of most foreign businesses in China and the expulsion of their staffs. In this political environment, Magnum photographers could not operate in China, and the recording of the first stages of China's new order was left either to the Chinese staff of government-controlled publications, or to technicians from the Soviet Union, who were particularly active and welcome in China during the Soviet-oriented First Five Year Plan for Chinese development from 1953 to 1957.

But for the years of 1956 to mid-1958 it is possible once again to get a sharp and emotive photographic record, through the photographs of Hiroshi Hamaya, and especially those of Marc Riboud, who produced a stream of photographs during his travels in China at this time. We know from the political record that this was a particularly difficult period for the intellectuals of China, who were encouraged by their leaders Mao Zedong and Zhou Enlai to speak out against abuses in the bureaucracy, and to suggest positive changes that could be made in China, only to be turned against by those same leaders and subjected to a humiliating 'anti-rightist' campaign in the summer of 1957. The 'investigations' made during this campaign led to the dismissals of hundreds of thousands of men and women – teachers, writers, journalists, artists – from their jobs, their separation from their families, and their assignment to poverty-stricken areas of the countryside, where they might learn from the peasants through constructive labour. Millions of other students and intellectuals, though not expelled or dismissed, were also marshalled for part time work in the nearby countryside, or in their own schools, campuses and work places. For the peasantry, at the same time, there was an equally major shift, since the state by late 1956 had decided to move from the post-land-reform system of cooperatives (in which peasant households received a return proportionate to the amount of land and draught animals that they contributed) to a collectivized system of agriculture, in which individual land rights would be surrendered, and family members recompensed in proportion to the work they performed in the common fields. By late 1958 this system was further concentrated by the Great Leap Forward into one in which all of China's agricultural land, along with the running of the educational, militia, and familial aspects of life, were to be centralized into a little over 20,000 enormous people's communes. Thus freed for constructive labour, Mao apparently believed, China's entire population of over six hundred million would be able to overcome all obstacles and march the country forward with new swiftness on the path to the Communist society.

The terrible bunglings and irrational programming that accompanied this 'Leap' are believed now by analysts to have led to the deaths from famine and other causes of twenty million people in China, but at the time no such crisis was publicly admitted. Instead, Mao, while stepping aside under criticism from some of his posts, continued to work to instill a passionate commitment to his version of socialist progress in the country at large. Once again it was Marc Riboud, his work supplemented this time by that of René Burri, who was able during visits to China in 1964 and 1965 to record this difficult period of retrenchment and ideological hyperbole. In 1966, as a faction claiming political and ideological affinity with Mao, and led by his wife Jiang Qing, launched the Cultural Revolution with its 'anti-feudal', 'anti-capitalist' and 'anti-Western' focus, the opportunities for Magnum photographers to work in China ceased, and once again the Chinese state photographers became the guardians of their own record.

What do the images of Riboud, Burri, and Hamaya tell us about the China of this time, a time of virtual isolation of the Chinese from the influences and pressures of the outside world? That isolation was certainly profound since the breaking of relations with the Soviet Union after 1960 was now added to the distancing from all things American that had been in effect since 1950. This was truly a time in which revolutionary changes were being attempted by China's leaders, and with the Communist Party already close to twenty million people in numbers one would expect dramatic evidence of the new society, or at least of its emerging foundations. But as we scan the photographs, we realize how hard such evidence is to capture. Without deep and intimate knowledge of the past realities, how can we truly gauge the depth, the nature or the meaning of the attempted change from the visual record? What we do get here, and often brilliantly or poignantly, is the sense of a country and a people with very little to rely on, where everything is scarce so everything is valued. The word poverty seems the wrong one, in the context, for to China's leaders – and surely to many of the people themselves after what they had been through – it was survival that was the first priority. Yet the paradox here was that the Great Leap brought not survival but death to millions. Hence the public expressions of ecstasy at national accomplishments, the cries of faith in Mao, seem strident and strained. We can only scan the faces held in position for us, and try to relate them to the canny face of Mao in Riboud's photo (48), or to the immense concrete statue of the leader, one arm raised in salutation above the belching smokestacks of the land he claimed to be reshaping (85).

At other levels, the images speak to us of ordinary things, of children and their games, of the quiet affections of age, of eating as shared relaxation. They speak also, insistently, of organization, of people in lines, of people listed, people marched to orders, people drilled. This the state was proud of, this the state allowed to be filmed, along with the work, the heavy manual work, whether of intellectuals or peasants, hacking endlessly at the heavy soil of China with mattocks and hoes, hauling barrows and sacks, pitting muscle against the land. So have farmers the world over laboured, but here the Chinese seem assembled in larger numbers than ever before, and their labour is in a context that is politically orchestrated.

In 1972, due to subtle shifts of view within the Chinese leadership that involved, among other things, the balancing off of new foreign policy directions in an attempt to curb the power of the People's Liberation Army, Mao Zedong invited President Nixon to China. With the breaking of the barriers to international tourism and the admission of China to the United Nations, even though the Cultural Revolution still continued in certain areas,

China was open to photographers on an unprecedented scale. Growing numbers meant decreasing state surveillance and control, and though certain military and strategic areas remained taboo, and many parts of China were still closed to foreigners, the images they caught grew in variety and frankness. Mao Zedong died in 1976, and the attempt of his chosen successor Hua Guofeng to develop his own cult – amusingly caught by Inge Morath in a 1978 photograph (101) – faded after a few years. From 1979, with the emergence of Deng Xiaoping as China's dominant leader, politics began to take a new direction, and the old days of Mao were over.

SPECIFICALLY, Deng and his associates decided to allow much greater contact between the United States and China, through full diplomatic recognition, student and cultural exchanges, and the encouragement of foreign trade and investment. Contacts with Western Europe and Japan were similarly expanded. In terms of the domestic economy, the commune system of controlled agricultural production in the countryside, geared to mandatory meeting of state grain quotas at fixed prices, was dismantled, and a new measure of individual incentive was allowed to individual farming families, working on a contract system. In urban industry, management's powers were greatly extended at the expense of party control, and a bonus system, graded wage scales, overtime, and dismissal for inefficient work were all permitted. With greater access to each other, farmers and urban purchasers moved to establish 'free markets' where prices would float to their 'natural' levels. The result, not surprisingly, was inflation, but also a dramatic rise in rural production as demand stimulated more work. Along with the spread of television and advertising, of foreign films and video cassettes, came changes in dating habits among the young, and a new freedom in dress and deportment. At last China, claimed Deng and his colleagues, along with certain Western journalists, was moving to the twenty-first century.

This dramatic transformation gave photographers – whether from Magnum or elsewhere – the kind of immediately vivid image of cultural change that proved evasive in the 1950s and 1960s, even though changes then had also been profound and far-reaching. But now the juxtapositions of cultures seemed immediate and amusing, as captured in Riboud's picture of a young couple carrying home their first TV set (132), or of startled Chinese tourists watching a Pierre Cardin fashion-show on the Great Wall, photographed by Eve Arnold (134).

Yet there is much that is baffling and inconclusive in this stage of China's history, not least in the arena of state control and individual freedoms. Section IV of this book starts, correctly one feels, with a photograph of the area outside the former imperial Forbidden City in Peking which, due to the frank posters displayed there in late 1978 and 1979, was given the hopeful name of Democracy Wall (116). It was indeed true that for a brief period these posters called dramatically and movingly for greater human freedoms in China, and for more participation by the people at large in the structures of government and in the selection of delegates for political conferences. But by the spring of 1979 the area of wall had been closed to posters, many of the writers of the original manifestoes had been jailed or silenced, and even the small underground magazines and journals that had helped fuel debate had been suppressed. Shortly thereafter, the right to post such public manifestoes was withdrawn from the constitution, and those who insisted on continuing to preach the message of the need for new freedoms – in film and visual arts as well as through writing – saw their works withdrawn by state censors and were themselves censured. It was in the early eighties that the government began to use the term 'spiritual pollution' as a term of blanket condemnation for those believed to be tainted by contact with, or influenced by, aspects of Western culture and philosophy. The search remained, as it had been so often in the later nineteenth century and in parts of the earlier Maoist period, for a Chinese scale of values that would derive technological and military skills from the West while still maintaining a Chinese 'essence' that was somehow true to the leaders' sense of cultural identity. In the nineteenth century this identity was to a Confucian scale of values; after 1949, to a Marxist one. When in 1986 several prominent scholars in China once again raised the issues of individual freedoms both in conscience and in scholarship, and were backed by student protestors, they were dismissed from the Communist Party and in some cases forbidden to teach or to give public lectures. Such a pattern of protest and political reaction is not easy to photograph, and does not appear visually in this volume, but it provides an undercurrent to many of the other more obvious images.

One other area, that is sharply shown in this section of recent Magnum photographs, is also worth a comment. The images of advertisements for Japanese electronic products (129) and Chinese thirst-quenching cola drinks (130), the billboards for romantic and historical film-shows (126), the gleaming new hotels (119) and the ranks of polished automobiles (120,121), the well-trained athletes beaming with ambition (139,140), do indeed represent a major change in the shape and direction of the Chinese culture and economy, and especially in the aspirations of urban life. Such changes have also, to a lesser but still marked extent, been gathering momentum in the countryside, where the families capable of earning ten thousand Chinese dollars a year are publicly extolled, and their entrepreneurial skills widely written up and emulated.

These successful men and women are building handsome new homes and accumulating formerly undreamt of amounts of personal possessions. Yet at the same time there are many – no one knows how many – who have been forced into bankruptcy or even to vagrancy by their failure to meet the local agricultural contracts that they successfully bid for in the past, or have been exposed to new hardships and hunger with the withdrawal of the state-provided cushion of grain procurement. Furthermore, the exploitation of teenage girls and young women, whether through marriage rackets or actual prostitution, has also been growing apace, in part as a response to the growing yet profoundly uneven patterns of new affluence. Those with wealth and local political clout are also often able to evade the tough one-child-per-family laws that the state feels obliged to impose now that China's population has climbed past the one billion mark. This in turn alienates those compelled to obey the law that militates against their basic love for large families, and also leaves them feeling dangerously vulnerable as they approach old age with neither adequate state pension schemes nor family members to sustain them. For these and many other reasons it seems correct to end this assemblage of Magnum photos with René Burri's quietly presented message of simplicity in the rural setting of Yan'an in 1986 (153) – a setting where fifty years before Mao Zedong sought to rally the spirits of the tattered veterans of the Long March, and to draft with their help his vision of China's future.

THUS we come back full circle to the images, allegedly of a 'timeless China,' with which this Magnum collection opens. There is no denying the beauty, and often the quiet power, of these images, several by the photographers already mentioned above, and others by Bruno Barbey and Thomas Hopker. Yet behind the beauty lies, in many cases, a pattern of mind- and body-breakingly hard work, and possibilities of human exploitation, that originally in the 1920s sparked the very emotions on which much of the rural revolutionary drives of the Communist Party were based. It is for this very reason that China seeks industrialization, electrification, mechanization of farm tasks, even if such changes may lead in turn to rural unemployment or a crisis in her international balance of payments. In a strange way, perhaps, this image of alleged timelessness should be paired with the statement that China is now preparing to enter the twenty-first century, suggested in the title to Section IV of the Magnum collection. For the danger may be that, despite all the sacrifice, the agony, the visions, and the sustained hard work that have been generated by the revolutionary process, and by the drives and passions of the Chinese people themselves, China is in fact only just now preparing, in many areas, to enter the *twentieth* century, with all the perils and anomalies that that implies. The Chinese people therefore will not soon be spared the harsh task of adapting to ever more complex technological standards, and of competing in markets where price levels are set by mechanized modes of production that further undercut the efforts of the human body, the one product that China has in supreme abundance. The Magnum photographers printed here have, in a myriad ways, shown the dignity, beauty, patience and tenacity of the Chinese people they encountered, and surely that counts for a great deal in history. But there is still something deeply sad about the tale they have to tell, something that lingers in the mind long after the pages have been closed.

1 Timeless China

Foreigners have been taking photographs of China for well over a century. As with people who discover China in other ways, everyone who approaches the country with a camera does so with a set of expectations and notions and is trying to find something. This has usually been an essential China, a 'real' China, an 'I was there' China. Unlike Chinese photographers, whose concerns are generally with subjects more specific than a whole country, a whole people or a whole culture, and also unlike the few resident foreign professional photographers who have made a living in China by working mainly for Chinese customers, the visiting foreigner is nearly always after Chineseness. The best of them also pursue a common humanity. These two aims are not in contradiction. Some visiting foreign photographers, such as Robert Capa in the 1930s, Henri Cartier-Bresson in the 1940s, Marc Riboud in the 1950s and 1960s, René Burri in the 1960s, or Inge Morath in the 1970s, have caught images that are both instantly recognizable as Chinese and give the viewer a feel for what it is like to be human in a particular time, place and set of circumstances.

Western travellers in China are rarely allowed to forget that they are foreigners and outsiders, especially when trying to understand the lives of the people all around. Yet this overwhelming human reality that is at the same time strange and familiar demands of the photographer that it be captured, recorded and reproduced. The very difficulty of doing this in China has imposed a realistic, reportorial photography on most of its visitors' cameras. The conspicuous foreigner who longs to be invisible, to blend into the crowd, wants to avoid imposing his or her personality on the pictures made. Few foreign photographers spend long enough in China to take 'Chineseness' for granted and be drawn into the kinds of approaches that make the viewer more aware of the photographer than the subject.

Visibility has always been a problem for the western photographer in China. It was of course worse in the nineteenth century, when the pioneer John Thomson reported that 'I frequently enjoyed the reputation of being a dangerous geomancer, and my camera was held to be a dark mysterious instrument which . . . gave me power to pierce the very souls of the natives, and to produce miraculous pictures by some black art, which at the same time bereft the individual depicted of so much of the principle of life as to render his death a certainty within a very short period of years.'

By the 1930s, when the earliest of the pictures in this collection was taken, the photograph was much more familiar, especially in the cities, and cameras were far less bulky and conspicuous. But the problem of being an intruder remained.

Sometimes the photographer's presence is very evident from the subject's curious or hostile response. We are at the same time aware of the intrusive photographer and of the victim's legitimate resentment at being caught in an undignified pose. It is to the photographer's credit when he brings home to us the ethical uncomfortableness of thrusting one's lens into other people's lives. In this, as with many of the other pictures in these pages, an affinity can be found with the photographers recording rural poverty with respect for human dignity in New Deal America. This is in keeping with the nature of the Magnum co-operative agency and its tradition of humanistic photography.

FOR MOST of the half century covered by this collection few Westerners visited China, and it was mainly through their still and moving photographs that people in Western countries formed their mental pictures of China. But there were not very many of these pictures easily accessible. Curiosity, where it existed, was generally combined with ignorance. Right up to the 1970s photographers could visit even the biggest cities such as Peking or Shanghai as explorers and discoverers venturing into the unknown. Sophisticates who would have blushed to photograph the Eiffel Tower or Buckingham Palace could see the Forbidden City with an innocent eye.

That period is now ending, and by the time this century is over so many Westerners will have visited China and so many television images will have been bounced around the world by satellite that there will no longer be much point in going to Peking and Shanghai just to take pictures. Photographers will go to cover news stories, to find 'undiscovered' corners, to make advertisements or to indulge in the sort of photography that depends on grants from foundations. As China joins the global village it becomes much harder to take a photograph there that means anything.

A THEME that recurs in Western photographs of China this last half century is the attempt to find an eternal, timeless China, a land where ancient traditions carry on unchanged, a people in closer touch with their own long past than Europeans or Americans are. Sometimes this theme has been set against another one; a country in the throes of revolutionary change, both before and after the establishment of Mao's new order in 1949. The first section includes some of the first group of images; most of the rest of the book illustrates change.

Here a word of warning must be put in. There is no more a timeless China than there is a timeless Italy or Japan. Hardly a picture in this first section could have been taken at any period other than when it was. From superficial details such as clothing to the changing structures of economic and social organization the processes of change have never stopped, even when at times they have slowed down. There has never been an unchanging China. There are not even many ancient buildings. Very few structures from before the fifteenth century survive except so thoroughly rebuilt as to bear little resemblance to their original forms. The man-made and man-destroyed rural landscapes have changed in all sorts of ways during a half century in which the population has doubled and the ways of life have been thoroughly shaken up several times over.

Even if some underlying values have changed less quickly than clothing styles or political and economic fashions, we must not assume that all is as it has ever been. To be sure, the family has emerged from the Maoist experiment with socialism a stronger unit than ever, but it is not quite the same as it was. Women are still less than equal with men, daughters less wanted than sons, but at least they nearly all have names now, and many learn how to write them.

AFTER the first section with its images of 'Chineseness' most of this book is organized by period. The second section covers the years of war from the 1930s to 1949. The third and largest part of the book is from the 1950s till the death of Mao in 1976, and the final section looks at the situation that has developed since then. This cannot give a representative set of images of China in a turbulent half-century or show all parts of the country. But these pictures can be offered as a selection of some of the best taken by foreigners in this period, and include classic images of China in the twentieth century that have defined China as a visualized reality in Western minds.

1 SOUTH CHINA'S RIVERS have been its arteries throughout history, and life has congregated along their banks. Here country people cross a river in Jiangxi on a bamboo trestle bridge. Before the era of the motor vehicle these structures – cheap, light and practical – were enough for all purposes. They could be built and rebuilt whenever necessary from local materials

2, 3 HUMAN MUSCLE is still often cheaper than animal or machine power. *Right:* trackers pull a boat upstream, wading through the shallow water. *Far right:* the image of China as it has been implanted on the Western mind – the Li River, composed like a Yuan landscape painting: mountains in the distance, a great expanse of water, and a tiny human figure on a raft in the foreground

4 IN THE SOUTH OF CHINA, where rainfall is enough to meet the demands of rice, the paddy-field landscapes have been maintained and worked for thousands of years under one of the world's most intensive agricultural systems. The main source of help to the peasants is the docile and hard-working water buffalo. Even at the height of collective farming, as when this group of Guangxi peasants and water buffaloes was photographed in 1965, rice cultivation remained essentially a small-scale process

5 NORTH CHINA FROM THE TRAIN WINDOW --
for the foreign visitor this is usually the first and
most vivid introduction to the texture of
Chinese life. This characteristic scene in
Northern China, with its carts pulled by
human and animal power, was taken from a
Peking – Canton (Guangchou) train in 1965

6 SHANGHAI has been for one and a half centuries the main meeting point of China and the West, and this applies to shipping too. The traditional sailing junk comes in a wide variety of designs to suit different conditions, as does the smaller single-sailed sampan. Before the Renaissance Chinese nautical technology was well ahead of Europe's, and contributed much to the West, including sail design, bulkhead construction, the balanced sternpost rudder, and the compass. Had internal political considerations not ended the distant voyages of Chinese fleets as far as Africa after the 1430s, it is probable that Chinese sailors would have rounded the Cape of Good Hope from the east before Vasco da Gama did from the west

7 SKILLED MONGOL HORSEMEN capture one of
the small but sturdy horses raised on the steppe,
using a loop on a long pole. Though the
Mongols are now outnumbered by Han
Chinese in Inner Mongolia, some of the
grassland still supports a pastoral way of life

8, 9   THE HALL OF PRAYER for Harvest (*left*) with its distinctive dark blue tiles is
at the north end of a broad stone-flagged causeway joining it to the Altar of
Heaven due south. It was used for an annual ritual by the reigning emperor in the
first lunar month, and is in the southern part of the former walled city of Peking.
Below: the palace city of the Ming and Qing emperors dominates central Peking.
The main buildings are set along a north-south axis. To the north was the *gong*,
the harem where the emperor lived with his women and eunuchs. To the south
was a series of halls used for state occasions separated by vast courtyards designed
to impress and intimidate. The main building in the picture is the Gate of Great
Harmony leading to the throne halls. Although both sites had visitors when
these photographs were taken in 1964, they were empty by the standards of the
tourist boom of the 1980s

10 A TYPICAL VILLAGE market in
Guangxi, photographed in 1965. China's
agriculture has long been commer-
cialized, and such markets survived
even the Great Leap Forward, albeit in
depressed form. During the 1980s rural
trade came back to vigorous life

11 THIS IS THE HOUSE next to the one where Mao was born in Shaoshan village, Hunan. His parents were rich peasants. The old woman knew him as a boy. The privilege of age grants mothers and grandmothers great powers over daughters-in-law and granddaughters-in-law. The traditional handicraft of spinning and weaving cotton at home was perpetuated by collective agriculture: peasants could not sell the raw cotton they raised on their tiny private plots, but they could process it for their own use

12, 13   No AREA OF LIFE is more sensitive than that of the family, and traditional values are not easily set aside. *Above:* the flying helmet marks the little boy off from the girl next to him in the kindergarten of a people's commune outside the ancient city of Luoyang. *Right:* not all children of working parents are entrusted to the care of the collective. Retired grandparents also look after the very young

14 A KAZAKH FAMILY in their tent in the far west of China. The Kazakhs form a distinct ethnic group, who are by long tradition nomadic herdsmen. Their nation has been divided by the Sino-Soviet frontier, and most now live in the Soviet republic of Kazakhstan, with fewer than a million remaining in China. Like other pastoral peoples of Central Asia, they value fine carpets that can easily be transported when they move their lattice-framed tents

15, 16 WORKING WOMEN. *Below:* the South Chinese way of fitting a baby to the mother's back; the cotton square with four broad bands is tied diagonally in the front. *Right:* an Uighur family in the grape-growing Turfan oasis of Xinjiang

17, 18 THE LONG PLAIT survives changes in fashion and ideology. The duties of an elder sister (*opposite*) can include carrying a younger brother when he demands it – a photograph taken in 1957 near the Yongehong (Lama monastery), Peking. In the 1980s (*left*) the traditional plait is worn with a modern shirt covered in foreign writing

2 Tides of war

THE CHINA that Westerners found in the 1930s and 1940s was a country at war. Since the end of the Qing dynasty in 1912 civil strife had been endemic. From the Japanese seizure of the Northeast (Manchuria) in 1931 onwards the very survival of China as a sovereign state was under threat, and in 1937 the country's warring factions came together in short-lived unity against what was now an all-out Japanese invasion. To most Western observers this paralleled the Spanish Republic's resistance to Franco, Hitler and Mussolini. As in Spain, the front soon turned out to be far from united; but when Helen Snow visited the Communist capital at Yan'an in May-September 1937 the Red Army was preparing to move from a truce with the Nationalists, their enemies in a decade of bitter warfare, to formally submerging its identity in the national army. For the veterans of the Long March this was not an easy thing to do, even though control of the former Red Army stayed in Communist hands.

The Japanese onslaught that began in July 1937 was met at first with fierce resistance by the armies of many different Chinese military groupings. In the Yangtse valley Chiang Kai-shek threw most of his best units into the battle for Shanghai, where the invaders were held up for three months at huge cost to the defence before they outflanked it and took Nanjing, Hangzhou and other cities, committing massacres of civilians that they did not bother to conceal from foreign observers. For a

while Wuhan was the focus of resistance till it too fell late in 1938, overwhelmed by the superior equipment, logistics and organization of the invader. Before the loss of Wuhan the armies of the Guangxi warlords had shown that 'little eastern foreigners' were not invincible in the long battle of Taierzhuang in southern Shandong. Although 1938 ended with Japan in control of many of the coastal, industrial and most fertile regions of China, China's resistance never collapsed; and her strategic defeats owed more to divided leadership and appalling logistics than to lack of willingness by her soldiers to stand, fight and die. The mood of 1937 and 1938 is well caught by the photographs of Robert Capa and Walter Bosshard.

For the next six years the war in China was strategically deadlocked. Neither Nationalists nor Communists could throw the invader out, but the prolonged war affected the two main Chinese factions very differently, weakening and corrupting the Nationalists and strengthening the Communists. In 1944 the Japanese came close to knocking the Nationalists out of the war; and it was only the Japanese defeats in the Pacific theatre that brought their advances in China to a halt. The Japanese surrender in August 1945 was followed by months of near war between Nationalists and Communists manoeuvring for advantage in the next conflict.

For Chiang Kai-shek, who had seen the forces of his bitterest enemies grow from tens of thousands in 1937 to over a million in 1945, the choice was between accepting Communist control of much of north China or trying to crush them militarily before they grew any stronger. As Mao and his colleagues were not going to surrender the war became open by the summer of 1946.

Within two years things were looking bad for the Nationalists from the Huai valley northwards. Because they had carried the war into their enemies' territory, where the Communists had won control of the great majority of the peasantry during the Japanese war and had since consolidated their position by organizing the redistribution of landlords' property, the Nationalists proved very vulnerable to the combination of guerilla and conventional warfare that was the Communists' strength.

In the winter of 1948-49 three huge campaigns destroyed Nationalist armies of about a million and a half men, leaving the way open for the victorious Communists to cross the Yangtse in the spring and press on south and west. Henri Cartier-Bresson spent nearly a year in China in 1948 and 1949, seeing the last weeks of Peking before its fall to the encircling Communists, watching the Nationalist armies abandon their capital Nanjing and the People's Liberation Army enter the city, and observing the beginning of the new order there and in Shanghai. He also spent several weeks in a Communist-held Shandong village, but was not allowed to keep the films he shot there, a great loss to posterity.

Nothing that has been written about the end of Nationalist rule in mainland China and the 'liberation' of the cities has ever matched the immediacy and actuality of Cartier-Bresson's photographs of one of the greatest political upheavals in twentieth century history.

These twelve years were the best of times and the worst of times. The Japanese war brought out both uncomplaining sacrifice by countless despised, underfed and badly led soldiers and, especially in its later years, selfishness and corruption among the Nationalist leaders of a grossness that appalled the most warhardened of foreign journalists. The civil war made the Nationalists even worse. By contrast the Communists found their role as defenders of the nation against the brutal foreign aggressors – a characterization that the Japanese military constantly lived up to – and as the only credible force that could rebuild China. Compared with the Nationalists they seemed straightforward and upright. During the Japanese war they put class struggle aside and flourished; and even during the civil war that followed the Japanese surrender their land

revolution was designed to create nothing more ambitious than a fairer small-peasant economy. Although the party kept the eventual achievement of socialism and communism in its programme, its greatest triumphs and highest popularity belong to this period when its immediate goals were patriotic and reforming. When the peasant armies of Mao Zedong and Zhu De marched into the cities in 1948 and 1949 most observers felt that at worst they would be a lesser evil than the Nationalists and that they offered a chance of making a new and better China. In 1948 and 1949 Mao looked to many like the saviour of China, and his victory like the end of a century of backwardness, disorder and foreign domination. The Nationalists, fleeing to Taiwan, appeared to be on the verge of extinction as a political and military force.

Forty years on the hopes and ideals with which the new order was founded are almost unimaginably remote, and the fervour has gone cold. These pictures bring back some hint of what it was to be alive and to be young before the revolution turned sour.

19, 20, 21 THE JAPANESE INVASION of July 1937 briefly united a country that had long been split by civil war. Mao Zedong's Communists joined with Chiang Kai-shek's Nationalists to resist the aggressors, though they retained separate commands. *Above:* three 'little devils' of the Red Army pose in Yan'an (Yenan) for Helen Snow in the summer of 1937 under the crossed flags of Soviet China and the Republic of China and the slogan 'Long live the liberation of the Chinese nation'. The torn paper poster calls for the realization of democratic rights. *Left:* boy soldiers of the Nationalist army in 1938. *Right:* a young Nationalist soldier ready for battle. His German-style helmet is a mark of the German influence in the Chinese armed forces in the 1930s

22 ZHU DE (1886-1976), the Red Army's commander in chief, addressing some of his men in Yan'an in June 1937 as they prepare to fight the Japanese alongside their former enemies, the Nationalist armies

23   A Red Army Unit on parade. Although poorly armed and equipped, the veterans of the Long March were the toughest and most determined soldiers in China

24 WHEN THE RED ARMY in north-west China joined forces with the Nationalists, it was redesignated the Eighth Route Army of the National Army. Though the Communists retained control over their own forces, they had to exchange the proletarian flat cap with a red star for the German-style slouch cap with the Nationalist white sun on a blue background. The troops drilling near Yan'an in 1939 are evidently from the Eighth Route Army; but as they are unarmed and include women they are probably not from a combat formation. The loess cliffs in the background can easily be tunnelled into to make comfortable dwellings, cool in summer and warm in winter

25 NATIONALIST OFFICER CADETS in the yard of their military academy, 1938. Their posture is part of an exercise to circulate the *qi* (ch'i, or vital pneuma). These exercises have thousands of years of tradition behind them in China, which made Western-style deep breathing techniques easy to accept. The basket and backboard have been essential furniture in any school yard or barrack square for well over half a century

26, 27 UNDER THE NATIONALISTS the Chinese Boy Scout movement was officially promoted in junior middle schools. Here a troop is taking part in an anti-Japanese demonstration in 1938. The poster at which the two boys are looking shows the sun of China shining over the White Mountain (Changbai shan) and Black River (the Heilongjiang or Amur) of Japanese-occupied North East China (Manchuria). On it is written:

The White Mountain smiles;

The Black River dances wildly.

Let us consign the years of rule by the Japanese bandits to the eastward-flowing stream

28 THE JAPANESE ARMY, vastly superior to
the Chinese forces in organization, supplies
and equipment, soon overran most of the cities
and main lines of communication in eastern
and northern China. Here they are seen
entering Hangzhou, the capital of Zhejiang,
in December 1937

29, 30   DURING 1938 Hankou became the headquarters of Chinese resistance.
The scene on the left shows the town still thriving and decorated with slogans in
support of Chiang Kai-shek. But by September it was being subjected to persistent
bombing raids from the air *(above)* and in October it too fell to the Japanese

31-34 CIVILIANS OF HANKOU under air attack, 1938. Although the Chinese people had been suffering ten years of civil war, Japanese airpower and firepower brought much worse devastation. No count could be kept of civilian casualties. But at first, to people not used to being bombed, air raids were a subject of curiosity more than fear

35 JAPANESE AIRPOWER devastated Chinese cities, bringing ruin and destitution to thousands. Here a woman weeps amid the shattered remnants of her home after a raid on Hankou, 1938

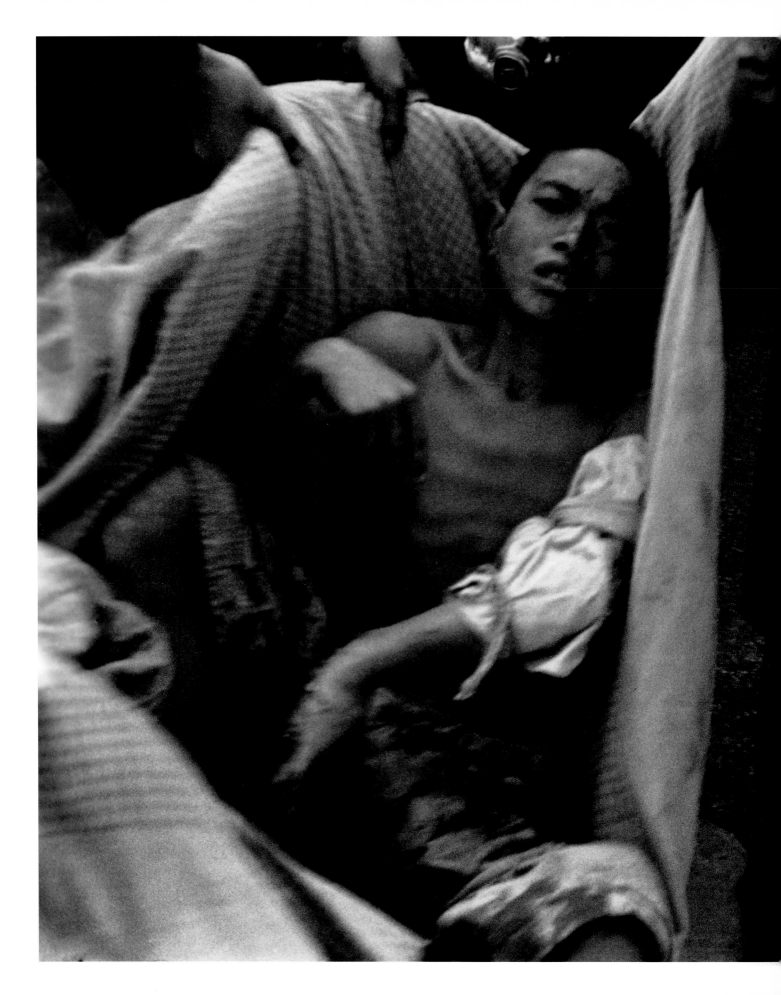

36 SOME OF THE BITTEREST FIGHTING of the war took place round Taierzhuang in southern Shandong. The Japanese launched their attack in March, 1938. They were met by the Fifth Route Army, mainly troops of the Guangxi warlords, who succeeded in inflicting heavy casualties. The Chinese claimed this as one of their few victories. The photograph showing a wounded Chinese soldier being evacuated was taken in April, 1938

37 THE CHINESE ARMY showed itself at its best at Taierzhuang. Here infantry advance across open country. Though news of the battle boosted morale, China was unable to exploit the victory

38　AN ARTILLERY OFFICER assesses the range of his guns at Taierzhuang

39, 40 TWO STYLES OF LEADERSHIP. *Left:* General Ma Hongkui (born 1893), the Muslim warlord controlling Ningxia and Qinghai in the northwest, visiting Chiang Kai-shek in Nanjing in 1948. According to Cartier-Bresson, 'he adored ice cream and had whole pails of it by him that he offered to visitors. Soon after this photograph was taken he was abandoned by his own troops.' He was later to take up ranching in southern California. *Below:* Mao (hands crossed) and Zhu De, the political and military leaders of the Communists, in Yan'an, summer 1937. Although the Chinese Communists have never advocated or practised egalitarianism, their leaders lived far more frugally than their Nationalist rivals before 1949

41 By 1946 the war against Japan was over. Communists and Nationalists resumed the civil war which had been suspended eight years before, and which ended in 1949 with total victory for the Communists. *Right:* outside Shanghai's railway station a senior Nationalist officer waits for a train to take him out of the beleaguered city. It is early spring, 1949, just before the troops of the People's Liberation Army made their entry

42 An old man (*far right*) is perhaps looking for a relative among the Nationalist recruits – some of the last to be mobilized – shortly before Peking surrendered to the encircling Communist forces on 31 January 1949. Though far from elegant, the soldiers' cotton padded uniforms were effective protection against the dry cold of the northern winter

43 WATCHED BY A WARY CROWD, the first
units of the People's Liberation Army enter the
Nationalist capital Nanjing. As the second
man is carrying a large cooking pot, this is no
doubt a cook squad. By the end of the year
Chiang Kai-shek's forces were utterly defeated
and he had left the mainland of China for ever

毛澤東主席

44, 45 THE NEW ORDER BEGINS, and Communist China assumes its soon to be familiar
face. *Left*: organized demonstrations in the Shanghai streets in the summer of 1949.
Students seem to be going through the motions of protesting against the continued
speculation in silver dollars that the city's new rulers were trying to suppress. *Above*:
trade-union members march with the already inevitable Mao portrait on 6th July to
celebrate the entry of the People's Liberation Army into the city at the end of May

3 Under Mao

ONE WAY of seeing the twenty-seven years from the proclamation of the People's Republic of China on 1st October 1949 to the death of Mao in September 1976 is as a tragedy. The country's Communist rulers, self-confident to the point of arrogance as a result of their extraordinary successes in seizing power from an initially much stronger opponent and in getting China back into shape during the first five or six years of the new order, try to transform human nature and even nature itself, refuse to hear reason, and thereby bring on disaster. What makes the tragedy dramatically less neat but in reality much more terrible is that the disaster falls almost entirely on the common people. To the end of his days Mao lived like an emperor: his punishment was only posthumous. Despite his attempts to ensure that his cause would outlive him, collective agriculture was to disappear within a few years of his death, and the young in whom he placed such hopes were to reject his values even more openly and enthusiastically than their elders.

Though the quarter century of Mao's China was overshadowed by tyranny and by the revolution's killings and famines, this period did see some remarkable transformations in China.

The first five or six years of the new order were some of the best, though they too had their dark side. Since the fall of the Manchu Qing dynasty in 1912 the people of China had suffered greatly from the absence of a central government strong enough to keep out foreign invaders and to prevent civil war, and the Communist leaders quickly established effective rule by the army-party dictatorship. A country that had faced extinction as a unified nation-state was now able to expel foreigners and to impose its control even over east Turkestan – still known by its nineteenth-century and blatantly colonial name of New Frontier (Xinjiang) – and Tibet; while in Korea its armies fought the United States and its allies to a standstill. These actions are all open to different interpretations, but to China's long-battered national pride they were a solace.

The economy too recovered during these years from the damage of decades of war. Inflation was brought down from astronomical rates to almost nothing. The redistribution of landlord property in the three quarters of the villages not previously under Communist rule strengthened the small-peasant economy based on tiny family farms; and though capitalists were intimidated, private industry and commerce flourished. Education spread; women acquired legal rights that were sometimes enforced; public health measures achieved striking successes. Though the years were marred by killings and persecutions, for most of its citizens life in the new China was decidedly better than under the old order. There was not much talk or thought of socialism.

By the winter of 1955-56 the Communist Party, itself barely ready for the plunge, was pushing the peasants into giving up their land for the untried benefits of collective farming; and soon afterwards private businesses were also socialized. In 1957 and 1958 those brave or foolish enough to accept the party's invitation to criticize its abuses of power were punished as 'rightists' in their hundreds of thousands, and everyone learned to keep quiet about their doubts from then on. So when Mao took up the idea that farming could be organized on a much bigger scale in people's communes, and that China's backwardness and poverty could be overcome with heroic efforts in a 'Great Leap Forward', few dared ask questions about the likely outcome of attempts to do the impossible. It soon turned out to be a leap into catastrophe. When a bold minority of his senior colleagues tried to tell Mao in 1959 that the policies were unrealistic and that the official figures of achievements were grossly exaggerated he turned on them and refused to ease off. Within three years starvation had taken some twenty to thirty million lives in what was possible the worst famine in Chinese history.

A retreat from extremism between 1962 and 1965 enabled China's economy to recover enough strength to face the next challenge to it, the misnamed Great Proletarian Cultural Revolution that lasted from 1966 to the death of Mao ten years later. The first three years of the Cultural Revolution were unprecedented: a Communist regime incited students and others to rebel against itself, kill chosen victims, help themselves to the army's weapons, and stage a multitude of local wars. The deaths have not been counted, but a million is a widely accepted estimate. The worst of the bloodshed was over by 1969, but under the late Maoist system of extreme autocracy clothed in socialist rhetoric China continued to miss out on development. Beneath the compulsory expressions of devotion lay a growing sense of dissatisfaction and resentment that found its outlet in such forms as the days of protest in Tiananmen Square in the spring of 1976.

Deeply flawed though the first quarter century of Communist rule was, and disappointed though many of the early hopes of the new order were, China did get back its national dignity and reacquire an identity in foreign eyes. Having expelled the Japanese and the Americans it also broke with the Russians, while keeping many Soviet institutions. Agricultural output barely outstripped the population explosion that Mao was unwilling to control, but industry grew many times over.

For a time it seemed that a new way of life had been created, a civilisation that put public and collective interests before selfish ones, a culture of simplicity and frugality symbolized by the blue cotton cap and jacket, the bicycle, and all-pervasive Maoist ideology. For some visitors from rich Western countries the experience of China in the Mao years was disturbing and oppressive; for others there was the temptation to seek in China a lost innocence. The visit could be the mental equivalent of a week or two at the fat farm before plunging back into the trough of sophistication, competitiveness, material plenty, and drugs and sex and rock and roll. The best observers, as can be seen in the pictures that follow, neither accepted nor rejected everything. There is behind all the photographs a pursuit of what it was really like to live in this alien but not inscrutable world. We cannot know what the faces we see would tell us if they could, but their eloquent silences invite us to guess.

Few foreign photographers were admitted to China during these years, and they were allowed to visit only a few places. What they saw of the countryside was restricted to the wealthier villages, nearly always those that enjoyed access to urban markets. Even the places where foreigners were allowed to wander off by themselves, feeling that they were exploring, were carefully chosen. The times when foreign photographers saw China were also controlled. There is nothing here from 1950-55, nothing from the worst starvation years of 1960-62, nothing from the violent phase of the Cultural Revolution. What we do have are some glimpses of a China that now belongs to the past, of ways of life that, before the Cultural Revolution at least, had an authenticity that the China of the Sony era cannot have. Yesterday's unmilitaristic army uniforms without insignia of rank had something that today's tawdry attempts at martial magnificence lack; and while the murderous excesses of the Cultural Revolution are well lost one can't help hankering after some aspects of a period when there was more to life than making money.

46 A PATROL of People's Liberation
Army soldiers in the streets of Nanjing
soon after the capture of the Nationalist
capital. Their straw hats are normal
peasant wear for working in the fields in
summer

47 CHILDREN QUEUE for rice *(opposite)*
in the winter of 1948-49. They belong
to a charity school which provided basic
education and food, run by the widow of
Sun Yat-sen, the leader of the Chinese
Revolution of 1912, who had died in
1925

48, 49   THE CONSOLIDATION OF POWER. Ten years after the establishment of the People's Republic of China, Mao (*left*) and his colleagues celebrated, though they had set the country on course for famine. At the National Day parade on 1 October, 1958 (*above*) Mao appears above Tiananmen, the Gate of Heavenly Peace, once one of the many imposing gateways on the main north-south axis of the huge palace complex of the Ming and Qing emperors in the centre of Peking. Under the People's Republic it was divided between a park, a museum, a cultural palace for the people, and a closed part reserved for China's new rulers to live and work in. The imperial Gate of Hevenly Peace was chosen as an emblem of the new state

50 IN THE EARLY DAYS life was still difficult, but for the urban poor it was an improvement on the old order. Except during the famines of 1960-62, the Communists nearly always provided registered city-dwellers with a modest but subsidized ration of grain and other bare essentials. This good humoured queue at a food shop is amused by the sight of the photographer

51 WESTERN DANCING was part of the Communist leaders' way of life in the Yan'an days, and this continued in the early years of the People's Republic. The stiff occasion above was held in the Summer Palace outside Peking on the eve of National Day in 1956. Later such dancing was to be condemned as bourgeois and disappear. It was revived in the 1980s, generally with a disco flavour

52 WHILE AN ARMY UNIT practising for the National Day parade on 1st October marches along the broad flagged terrace that joins the Hall of Prayer for Harvest (seen in the background) to the Altar of Heaven in the southern part of Peking, an old man thinks his own thoughts

53 SPECTATORS watching street entertainers, 1957. Again, some of them obviously find the foreign photographer more interesting than the show they are supposed to be watching

54 To HAVE ONE'S PICTURE put up on
the honour board of advanced workers
at the gate of one's factory was in the
early decades of the new order a coveted
distinction. By the 1980s such honours
mattered less than financial incentives

55 TRAINS have been the main
method of long-distance travel in China
throughout the four decades of the
People's Republic. Accommodation is
of four classes, of which hard seats (as
here) is the cheapest. The ability of
strangers to become a temporary
community on a long train journey
makes such travel much more agreeable
than one might expect in the physical
conditions. Luggage racks are usually
very full. This train is in Xinjiang, and
most of the passengers clearly Uyghurs

56 MAO'S DISLIKE OF INTELLECTUALS who
would not get their hands dirty was visceral. A
minor but healthy byproduct of the fervour of
the early phases of the Great Leap Forward, a
campaign that was to be fatal to tens of millions
of peasants, was the involvement of university
students in manual labour. This young woman
was taking part in the building of a new
swimming pool for her University in 1958

57, 58 RELIVING THE PAST. Yan'an (Yenan) in northern Shaanxi, an old frontier garrison town controlling the northern approaches to the great city of Chang'an (modern Xi'an), was the Communist capital from 1936 until it was evacuated during the civil war in 1947. Though no longer a power centre thereafter, it was treated as a shrine of the revolution where pilgrims visited the sacred sites, especially during the Cultural Revolution, when the most devout marched there on foot. The youngsters (left) are climbing the Pagoda Hill that dominated the town and the valley of the Yan river. University students (above) are working on a dam

59, 60 Vegetables, poultry and other cash crops are generally more profitable to raise than grain where there is access to urban markets. The woman and girl are loosening the soil and weeding with long-handled multi-tined hoes that do the same sort of job as a gardener's fork – without the benefit of solidly shod feet. Both pictures were taken in the outskirts of Shanghai, 1964

61, 62 THE COLLECTIVE AGRICULTURE of the people's commune generally
involved traditional farming methods organized on a larger scale. The women
carrying hoes (below) were going to or from work in the outskirts of Shanghai.
The machinery to the left is transplanting rice seedlings that have been started
off in small seedbeds while the main paddy-fields were still growing the previous
crops. Transplanting was traditionally backbreaking work. Much simple farm
machinery was developed during the Great Leap Forward years

63   THE VIETNAM WAR brought the People's Republic into indirect conflict with the United States. In the middle sixties China increased both its aid to Vietnam and its preparations for possible direct military intervention. A Chinese army unit works near Nanning, the capital of Guangxi, to widen a road to carry supplies to Vietnam. In 1979 this road was doubtless one of those used in the Chinese invasion of Vietnam

64, 65 STUDENTS from the 1950s to 1970s lived frugally, dressing as simply as possible, and sharing crowded dormitory rooms that might hold eight hard bunks around the walls. The bunk was the nearest thing to a space of one's own; but even that had to serve as a seat for room-mates and visitors if it was a lower one. (Note the Stalin pin-up: his cult continued in China long after he was denounced by Nikita Khrushchev in the Soviet Union.) Even a graduate like this Shanghai specialist (left) working in a Kunming ball-bearing factory still shares a dormitory room

66, 67 THE MOST POPULAR READING in China has long been 'little people books', illustrated comic books – a picture a page, the story written underneath, and no speech bubbles. These comics will have been rented from a tiny street library for one cent a copy, to be read on the spot, stools provided by the owner of the collection. Peking Library, China's National Library (*below*), provided a free service for its readers in its mock-traditional building next to Bei Hai Park

68, 69   YOUNG PIONEERS with their red scarves were the Communist Party's answer to the Scouts. Not all children were allowed to join: a 'bad' class background made it hard to get in before entry was thrown open in the 1980s. The parade with wooden rifles *(below)* was photographed in Changchun in 1965, and the singers in Shanghai *(right)* in the previous year

70, 71   MASS DEMONSTRATIONS in the big cities were highly organized affairs.
Work units and schools were told how many people each should field, and even
temporary extra public conveniences were installed along the route. The crowds
seen here in front of the Gate of Heavenly Peace were on their way to the North
Vietnamese embassy to demonstrate in favour of Vietnam and against the United
States, which was then teaching the world the new term 'escalation', as it
stepped up its military intervention in South Vietnam and bombed the north. It
was widely expected in China that before long Chinese forces would be entering
the Vietnam War

72, 73   A WEDDING between two employees at a Peking textile mill in January, 1957. These two photographs *(left)* show celebrations in a school classroom after the ceremony. The groom is a manager from the north, the bride a worker from the south. Hanging on the wall is an inscription that reads: 'Strengthen solidarity between staff and workers to make a go of the enterprise; North and south united to produce by day and night'

74   DIVORCE is legal but not easy to obtain. In this 1965 case, the wife contested the petition and the husband was refused the divorce he asked for. The judge is sitting second from the left, flanked by two assessors and a clerk. The same portrait of Mao presides over the joining together and the putting asunder

75, 76 MOTHERHOOD: two photographs taken in a Peking maternity hospital in 1965. Improvements in public health, especially in the cities, have been one of the People's Republic's greatest achievements. By later standards the attitude to population control was still very relaxed, and three or four children were not thought of as a large family

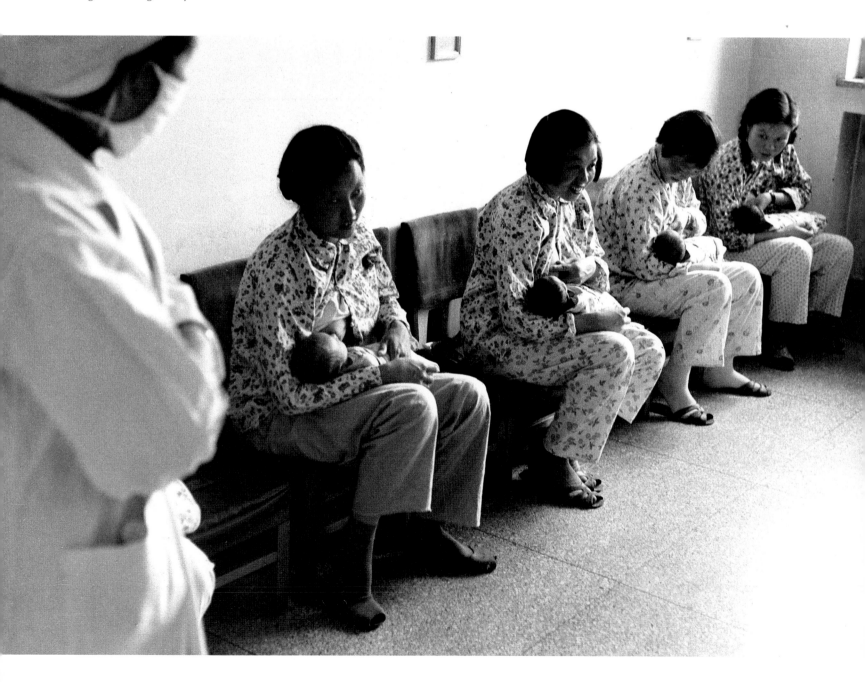

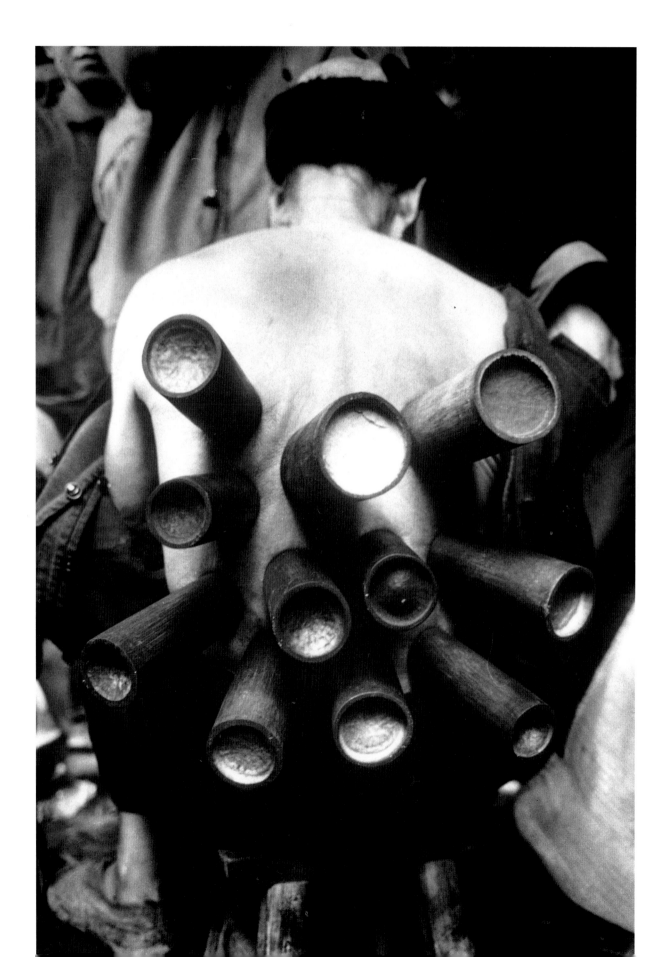

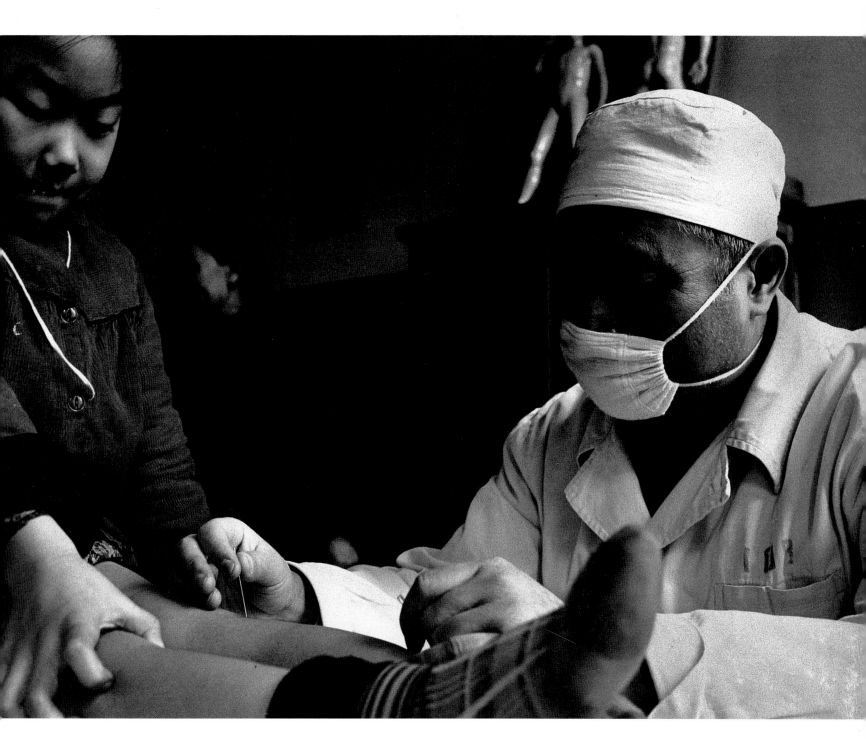

77, 78 CHINESE MEDICINE has a long, rich and well-recorded tradition, based on restoring the correct balance between the vital forces in the whole person. Under the People's Republic this tradition has been combined with Western medicine. *Left:* a man being cupped with sections of bamboo on a market day in Guilin in 1980. *Above:* a child receiving acupuncture treatment. The doctor twiddles the needle to send a stimulus along one of the many lines of force that are thought to join different parts of the body. Although the effectiveness of acupuncture in treating many conditions is empirically established, Western-style scientists have yet to find a fully satisfactory explanation of how this happens

79 THE CONVIVIALITY of the family meal, in which each member eats from the common dishes, is at the heart of Chinese social life. A group such as this photographed in 1964 might, with slight variations in clothing styles, have been seen at any time in the last thousand years

80 EATING is a serious business in China, and an occasion for the family – often several generations – to come together. In 1964 the familiar image of Chairman Mao watches over this Shanghai dining table. The little girl is no doubt a neighbour

81-83 STREET SCENES of the sixties. These photographs are a reminder of how little traffic there was even in the biggest cities. *Below:* Peking in 1965. The white wooden box on wheels in the foreground contains ice-lollies, sold for five cents each. *Right:* two views of the Nanjing road, Shanghai's busiest shopping street. The woman and child are probably moving garbage. The tricycle carriage or pedicab was a more humane replacement for the rickshaw pulled by a running man

84, 85 AIR POLLUTION was a consequence of the rapid industrialization and urban
growth that began in the 1950s, and was due mainly to the burning of large quantities of
dirty coal, which turned Peking's sky from clear blue to hazy grey. *Above:* in the grounds
of Peking University. The pagoda is a water tower. *Right:* the smoking factory chimney
behind a giant statue of Mao symbolizes one side of his vision for China's development:
massive investment in industrial might under autocratic rule. The other side was small-scale
technology and mass participation. Few of the concrete Mao statues seem likely to
survive the twentieth century: by the late 1980s they were already being dismantled

86   PRIVATE ENTERPRISE: the old man selling mugs of tea in a Peking street in 1957 was practising one of the few kinds of private business then permitted to exist; it was too small-scale to be socialized

87, 88   STATE RETAILING: in the 1950s and 1960s the state ran an efficient food supply
system for the cities. The stall on the left is in Shanghai, on the right in Peking. Vegetables
were cheap and plentiful; meat and fish more expensive and subject to rationing

89, 90   AN INGENIOUS HYBRID of Chinese chess and billiards. The pieces are
discs with names incised on the top – general, minister, soldier and so on, and
they move along lines, propelled by cues, instead of on squares. *Below:* the 'Great
Wall of China Game', a popular children's game, here played in a Peking street
in 1964

91 TABLE TENNIS has become virtually the national sport of modern China, though challenged by volleyball, basketball and, more recently, soccer. Only minimum space and equipment are needed. It is on slabs of concrete such as these in a Peking schoolyard and countless tables in corridors and club rooms that China's many world champions have made their start

92, 93 THE ARMED FORCES assumed a particularly important place in nearly all walks of life after the Cultural Revolution had created power vacuums that only they could fill. The soldiers (*opposite*) are turned out at Peking Airport in 1973 to welcome a foreign dignitary. At that time there were no visible distinctions of rank, except that officers had four pockets on their tunics while the rest had only two. That same year Shanghai turned out an honour guard of its People's Militia, including these women (*left*) wearing outfits that were surely chosen and issued by the authorities for their theatrically proletarian effect. It was said later that the Shanghai militia was intended to be part of the backing for Jiang Qing's faction in the struggle for power after Mao's death (see pl. 101). In the event Shanghai was as glad as the rest of the country to see the fall of Jiang Qing and her associates

94, 95 TEN HUGE BUILDINGS designed in an undistinguished Western-influenced style were erected in Peking in 1958-59, and Tiananmen Square was vastly enlarged to be a setting for mass rallies. Beside the square was one of the biggest of the ten monsters, the Great Hall of the People, seen above through the massive portico of another, the joint Museums of Chinese History and of the Chinese Revolution. The soldier on the left is one of the many uniformed and plain-clothes guards posted around the Great Hall on special occasions to keep the people out

96, 97 THE ACROBATIC TRADITION, often featuring almost unbelievable feats of balance, goes back at least two thousand years, and has long been used to impress foreign visitors who cannot be expected to appreciate the 'higher' forms of culture: early in the 15th century a Persian embassy was so entertained when it crossed the Ming frontier. Behind the breathtaking performances such as the one on the left in Shanghai in 1964 lie lifetimes of dedicated training. A moment of this caught on the right in 1956

98   STATUES OF MAO, often with his right hand raised in an inspirational but remote gesture, appeared all over China in the late 1960s. The idols were designed to very strict specifications from the party authorities, and they had to be treated with the greatest respect. This one was seen in a theatre in 1971

99, 100   WESTERN-STYLE BALLET was pressed into ideological service by Mao's wife Jiang Qing. *The White-Haired Girl* was originally a simple drama about a young village woman whose hair turned white after she fled from the oppression of a landlord. In the scene *(centre)* she is being saved by the Communist army.

The dancer practising *(right)* is possibly rehearsing the scene of an escape from prison in the first famous revolutionary ballet, *The Red Detachment of Women,* celebrating in extremely fictionalized form the exploits of women Communist guerillas on Hainan Island in the 1930s

101 AGITPROP ART accounts for a large proportion of works produced in the People's Republic, often reflecting changes of policy or personalities. In October 1976, two weeks after Mao's death, the undistinguished apparatchik Hua Guofeng staged a coup d'état that put Jiang Qing and her closest associates in jail and raised him to supreme power. Although he tried to look like Mao, even to the hairstyle, he succeeded only in resembling North Korea's Kim Il Sung. Here his standard portrait is being programmed for jacquard silk looms in Hangzhou in 1978. A few months later Hua was on the way out; but, unlike Mao, Deng Xiaoping spared his rival from the cruder forms of public humiliation

102 CHINESE IS NOT AN EASY SCRIPT to learn. Although illiteracy was greatly reduced in the early years of the People's Republic through adult classes such as the one in which the country woman above is learning to use the traditional writing brush, a large minority of village women are still unable to read and write. This woman, however, is successfully acquiring a kind of power hitherto denied her

103 THE JAPANESE CONDUCTOR Seiji Ozawa, born forty-four years earlier in the Japanese-occupied Chinese city of Shenyang (Mukden), toured China with the Boston Symphony Orchestra in 1979. The novelist Zhou Erfu is here writing an honorific scroll about worldwide fame for the conductor's mother

104 THE GENERATIONS of a family seem almost to belong to different historical periods. Here, in Peking, 1964, the young man reads the *China Youth News*, but his grandmother is busy with an immemorial female task: sewing together many layers of old cloth to make the sole of a cotton shoe. Such shoes are very comfortable but need frequent replacement

105 BEFORE THE AGE OF MASS TOURISM, in 1973, a family visit the Summer Palace outside Peking. They have the look of southerners

106 THE NEW MUCH-VISITED and very crowded stretch of the Great Wall at Badaling outside Peking is only a few centuries old and was rebuilt in the 1950s. Since this picture was taken in 1971 another stretch has been recreated to accommodate the demands of the tourist industry, and this historic obstacle to contacts between nations has been used in official propaganda as a symbol of Sino-foreign friendship

107, 108   THE GIANT PANDA is an endangered species, and the Chinese
authorities have exploited the interest that the rest of the world takes in its fate.
But while Western nations worry about the panda and pay for its attempted
rescue, there is no concern for the Qiang tribespeople moved from their home
villages in attempts to preserve its habitat. *Left*: Peking Zoo, 1965. *Above*:
Chengdu Zoo, the nearest zoo to the remaining panda homeland

109, 110 Two HOUSEHOLD SHRINES of the 1960s. The central, dominant
position is taken by the chairman, flanked in the lower one by exhortations to
study Chairman Mao and build a new China. Family photographs are much
smaller, except for those of dead paternal ancestors

111 BEHIND THIS RETIRED COUPLE are pictures of them in their youth as soldiers
of the Communist Party's Eighth Route Army during the war against Japan of 1937-1945

112, 113 YOUNG COUPLES are restrained in public by Western standards, especially when foreigners are looking. Open displays of affection are considered indecorous, one reason for the official disapproval of 'decadent' Western films, books and videos

114, 115 SMALL CHILDREN, on the other hand, are indulged in every way, including being allowed to relieve themselves almost anywhere, as on the steps of this Peking shop (*above*). The baby in the back of the three-wheeler truck (*left*) has perhaps just been lifted out of the bamboo baby-walker to the right

4 Towards the twenty-first century

I T TOOK MORE than the coup d'état of October 1976 – that put four of the closest associates of the late dictator's declining years behind bars less than a month after his death – for the Mao era to end. For the next two years the new party chairman, Hua Guofeng, maintained the forms and much of the essence of the previous period. Only in the last months of 1978 was his main rival, Deng Xiaoping, strong enough to take power from him and begin the historic demolition not only of the policies of the Cultural Revolution decade but also of almost everything else that had been done since 1955. Deng, like many other officials, had been attacked and humiliated during the turbulent phase of the Cultural Revolution, had come back to senior positions in the early 1970s, and had been thrown out again by the Maoists early in 1976. It was thus hardly surprising that he moved fast to have the Cultural Revolution anathematized. Given the rough treatment he had received from Mao it was only natural that he should have encouraged the steady down-grading of Mao, especially of his later years. But the ending of collective agriculture, the foundation of Chinese socialism, was a much more fundamental change. This implied that the rural policies of the previous quarter of a century had been wrong, and that the people's communes were in such a bad way that nothing short of their abolition was going to save China's agriculture. Thus it was that in the early 1980s the family small-holding leased from the state became the normal farming arrangement, and peasants worked for themselves and for money instead of for officials and work points.

Discarding Mao's murky but potent doctrine of the primacy of class struggle and writing off rural socialism was a dangerous move that risked undermining the party's raison d'être. Deng also took on the armed forces, humiliated as they were by their inability to stage a quick and effective invasion of Vietnam in 1979, cut their budget and their size, and defied them to mount a coup if they dared. As if this were not enough he staked the economy's future on getting growth by pumping money into the countryside through higher procurement prices while hoping to be able to keep the consequent inflation under control. By the late 1980s the main obstacle to further economic reform lay in the massive state-owned industrial system and the bureaucracy that ran it. If it was to be made as efficient as it might be there would have to be unemployment on an alarming scale, not only of workers and technicians but also of an army of officials who contributed little or nothing to output. Although the bankruptcy of state-owned enterprises was made possible and in the occasional well-publicized case actually happened, moves towards breaking the iron rice bowl of lifelong job security were slow and cautious.

Economic change extended to foreign trade too. The old policy had been a very cautious one of incurring as few international debts as possible, of minimizing Chinese dependence on foreign suppliers and markets, and of avoiding the dilution of sovereignty that would have been the consequence of accepting foreign investment: foreign-owned businesses had been taken over in the 1950s. Under Deng China became eager for foreign loans, multiplied foreign trade many times over so that China is now inextricably involved in the world economy, and encouraged foreign firms, including the big multinationals, to invest in China on terms that involved many concessions by the host country.

As China became one of the world's tourist traps it also lost some of its superficial exoticism for Westerners, not in itself a bad thing. Soon it will no longer be possible to publish a book about China on the strength of a three-week visit; and one day it may even be normal for foreign journalists to be competent in the language.

China became ideologically less exotic in the 1980s. In order to launch his reforms Deng had dumped some dogmas and encouraged greater freedom of expression, although the limits of his tolerance could sometimes be sharply contracted. The problem for the authorities was how far they could go in allowing criticism of the system. If party secretaries no longer control the economy, if foreign ideas have so strong an influence on the young, if the institutions of party rule are undermined by discussion of other possible arrangements, if socialism is treated openly as a bad joke, if money is all-powerful, then the rulers depend more and more on carrots and sticks to maintain control. This is dangerous and disturbing to those who remember a time when the party also commanded respect.

Given this uncertainty at the top, the 1980s saw a revival of Chinese culture led by the generation of young city-dwellers who had been Red Guards during the late 1960s, had been exiled to the countryside or remote frontier districts, and had made their way back to the cities toughened mentally and physically and utterly disillusioned. Their youthful ideals had turned sour, and they wanted to make sense of their lives after being forced to waste their youth. In writing, popular music, film and the other visual arts new talent burst out of the old restraints, and what it lacked in subtlety and formal education it made up for with its energy, courage and openness. In clothes, hairstyles, forms of speech and other ways many more young people drew a line between themselves and the revolution's traditional values. As the persecution of religions was eased it emerged that the numbers of believers in China's many faiths had increased under Mao. Buddhist and Taoist temples, mosques and churches were thriving.

In other areas the iron fist of the proletarian – now renamed people's democratic – dictatorship was used with fewer inhibitions. Outright dissent was punished with long terms of imprisonment. The disturbing rise in crime was met with a draconian policy of multiple executions in every urban centre several times a year, while young people were sent to the Gulag of the far west by the hundred thousand. Even according to official figures this ruthlessness has not had much success. Harsh measures intended to slow down the alarming growth of China's population worked in the cities, where the one-child family became the norm, but were much less effective among the peasant majority, whose greater wealth and freedom enabled many of them to get round the rules. The shadow of ecological catastrophe grows darker as less and less arable land has to feed some ten million extra mouths each year.

AFTER A DECADE of Deng's reforms it could seem at some times that everything had been changed and at others that nothing was really different. The weight of tradition still pressed heavily down on people's minds and lives, and Westernization was often only superficial. And yet China was at the same time a society in economic and intellectual ferment, in which all values were open to question in private if not in public, in which what ten years earlier people would scarcely have dared to think could now be said, in which foreign influences made themselves felt in many different ways. Even if one knew what the rules were, there could no longer be confidence that they would hold a few years later. After a decade of the unthinkable happening, after a tremendous economic gamble that had paid off for most people, after so many changes carried out without provoking great disorder, it was becoming possible to hope that China would enter the nineteenth century before the twentieth was over.

116 AFTER MAO'S DEATH in
September 1976, his successor Hua
Guofeng tried to continue many of his
policies despite growing pressure for
reform, but Hua was unable to silence
demands for change indefinitely. For a
few months in late 1978 and early 1979
the handwritten poster and the privately
mimeographed pamphlet and magazine
were allowed to flourish and express a
little of the discontent felt in society.
This served Deng Xiaoping in his
struggle to impose his reformed
dictatorship. A national focus for the
democracy movement was a stretch of
wall near the Xidan crossroads on
Chang'an Boulevard in Peking where
posters could be put up and magazines
sold: this is the 'Democracy Wall' seen
in the spring of 1979 below. The readers
do not talk to each other or reveal their
reactions: anyone might be connected
with Public Security. Soon afterwards
Deng first restricted then suppressed
these Maoist rights of protest that had
ceased to serve his needs. The more
obstinate magazine editors were jailed,
and the historic wall was hidden behind
glass-fronted advertising hoardings, an
appropriate symbol for the 1980s

117, 118, 119 To the Western world China today presents a face that is
alien both to itself and to its visitors. Shanghai's Peace Hotel (*above left*) may still
retain some traces of its raffish elegance as the Cathay Hotel of the interwar years.
It is hard to say the same for Pierre Cardin's Maxim's in Peking (*lower left*), a
luxury restaurant with as little connection with Chinese life as possible. Another
1980s joint venture with foreign capital is the Great Wall Hotel (*above*), sited in
a dreary expanse of Peking suburbs, looming oppressively over the little
apartment blocks that surround it

120, 121, 122   GLIMPSES OF A DYING
ERA: cities in 1978 on the eve of the
beginning of Deng's reforms. *Above left:*
two of China's own hand-built
limousines for senior officials waiting
outside a Shanghai department store.
The Red Flag cars have now mostly been
replaced by imported Mercedes-Benz
models. *Below:* cars – mainly old Soviet
Volgas – for foreign visitors and business
people outside Peking's Nationalities
Hotel. The vehicles now would be
Toyotas. The private car remains far
outside the reach of almost every
ordinary Chinese. *Right:* the Bank of
China in Shanghai, covered with
slogans celebrating the twenty-ninth
anniversary of the People's Republic

123 CITY HOUSING was badly neglected during the last twenty years of Mao's rule. So little was spent on it, despite rapid urban population growth, that even according to official figures there were only about four square metres of living space per head in the big cities, leading to appalling overcrowding for all but the privileged few. Thus the mushrooming of cheaply-built and generally ugly apartment blocks in China's cities and towns since the late 1970s has been a desperately needed alleviation of a hunger for homes. A block such as this in the southern city of Guilin (Kweilin), with a section of balcony for each family and the balconies remarkably uncluttered, would be highly desirable

124   THE SMALL ISLAND of Shamian (Shameen) in the Pearl River in the middle
of Guangzhou (Canton) was for a century a foreign-ruled enclave. Its handsome
colonial buildings have been largely refurbished to make the island a peaceful
tourist spot, though its history has contained a number of violent episodes.

125   IN OLD AGE those who have worked for the state continue to receive a high
proportion of their pay after retirement, while the peasant majority depend on
family or the charity of the village. These retired men enjoying the warmth of
Peking's winter sun probably have the security of pensions

126 GIANT FACES overlook more old men sunning themselves in Peking in 1980. The film advertised is *Child from Overseas*, a melodramatic prize-winning production from Canton's Pearl River Studio

127 HANDPAINTED HOARDINGS in Shanghai advertising local products, the one on the left being for Dadi raincoats and jackets. When this picture was taken in 1982 city people were only just beginning to emerge from Maoist uniformity of dress: the necktie was then quite a daring symbol of Westernization

128 CHINESE BUS STOPS, like this one outside the Great Wall Hotel in Peking, carry the name of where they are as well as the route number and destination of the buses that stop there. At rush hours the buses are extremely crowded, and getting on or off them is a physical struggle

129 WHERE THE IMPERIAL JAPANESE ARMY failed the big Japanese companies
are succeeding. Hoardings that once carried pictures of Mao and quotations from
his works now serve the all-conquering yen. The Chinese text of this Sony
advertisement in central Peking proclaims 'Sony hopes to be of all-round service
to Chinese friends through these products'

130   CHINA IN THE 1980s has joined the Coca Cola world system, even serving the
product at state receptions and banquets. But in a culture that still takes a relaxed
approach to trade marks, plenty of local state-run soft drink companies have produced
rivals, such as Shanghai's Lucky Cola here advertised on a Shanghai street. The familiar
bottle shape is no coincidence

131, 132 TELEVISION AND AUDIO EQUIPMENT became widely available in the late 1970s. Prices are still high, compared with average salaries, but shops, such as this state-run store in Wuhan, are quite well stocked, with Japanese as well as Chinese goods. At the time this young couple were triumphantly carrying home their new set from Wangfujing, Peking's main shopping street, in 1979, the era of mass television was just beginning for China. Within less than ten years there was a black-and-white set in most city homes and a colour one in a growing minority of them

133, 134   A PRANCING MODEL using the Great Wall as backdrop
evokes smiles of embarrassment as well as interest from spectators.
Pierre Cardin's was one of the first Western fashion houses to produce
in China, and his clothes are being displayed in this 1984 picture.
Chinese tailors in the 1980s were quick to adapt foreign fashion to
local tastes. *Below:* a market in the province of Jiangsu

135, 136 THE FRUGAL WEDDINGS of the Mao era (see pls. 72, 73) are now things of the past. If expense is spared, the young couple will look cheap. Instead of having wedding photographs taken at the legal ceremony or the reception a couple will often visit a photographer's studio. Here it is often possible to hire Western clothes, including a bridal outfit, or as much of it as will be seen in the picture

137, 138 OLD-FASHIONED one-piece swimsuit and cheap plastic sandals look good on this Qingdao (Tsingtao) boat racer (*left*). *Below*: showing off the new Honda and US-style gear at Leshan in the western province of Sichuan. On the suspension bridge in the background, a traditional style suited to the valleys of the west, porters still carry their loads on their backs.

139, 140 CHINA TAKES ITS PLACE on the stage
of international gymnastics

141 NOT ONLY FOREIGN TOURISTS have flocked to the famous sights of China in their millions in the 1980s. This state-owned souvenir shop is just inside the Badaling stretch of the Great Wall outside Peking

142   AT MOST TOURIST SPOTS one can hire a camera, buy a film, and get it developed on the spot. The decision on which negatives to have printed can be made after returning home. These young tourists are examining their black-and-white pictures of their trip to Xindu, a town to the north of Chengdu

143 CYCLES OF CATHAY. Most commuters in Peking get to and from work by pedal power, and the number of bicycles on the road is constantly growing. At rush hours, the flow is so dense that barriers are now put up on the middle of each side of Chang'an Boulevard to stop the cyclists from taking over the whole width of the road. Few riders give hand signals or look behind them before turning, and lights are rarely used after dark. Now that the number of motor vehicles sharing roads with them is increasing rapidly, cyclists make up a large part of the annual 700 or so deaths on Peking's roads. This photograph was taken at 6.30 am one morning in 1979

144, 145   THE RAISING OF PET BIRDS has, like so many traditional customs that came under attack during the Cultural Revolution, revived since 1976. Cage birds are particularly popular with retired people, and unlike most other pets have not been banned in the cities. The birds on the left, which appear to be on sale, are by a street in Chengdu. The bird above was being sold in Peking in 1982, when such private trading was still only just tolerated by the authorities

146   THE COMMUNAL EXERCISES that impress and often surprise visitors to China
form part of schoolchildren's daily programme

147 MASSAGE ROUTINES for the eyes are believed to improve eyesight. These
youngsters are in a Shanghai middle school

148, 149, 150   People perform their exercises wherever there is a convenient
space. *Above left:* a woman stretching one morning in a park in the province of
Hubei. *Below left:* the wide pavements by the north gate of the former palace
in Peking can also be put to good use, not only for stretching exercises but
also for practising musical instruments or reciting one's lessons. *Above:* for
older people *taijiquan*, once a form of training for unarmed combat, has become
a fairly gentle form of keeping fit, seen here in the park surrounding the Altar of
Heaven in Peking

151   TAIJIQUAN'S ORIGIN in unarmed combat is more obvious in the case of this young woman exercising (for the cameraman, perhaps?) in Shanghai in 1978

152   A LIFE CLASS at the Chongqing Academy of Fine Art. Although Mao once sanctioned the use of nude models in art education, traditional Chinese values equate portrayal of the naked body with obscenity. In the 1980s life classes have been uneasily restored

153   BUT IN THE COUNTRYSIDE of the north-west there are few signs of Westernization: the clothes are much as they might have been ten or twenty years earlier. Country bicycles are specially strengthened to withstand bad roads and heavy loads. This crowd was waiting at a bus stop along the road to Yan'an (Yenan) in 1986

Chronology

1911–12 Nationalist and republican revolution leads to abdication of Pu Yi, last emperor of Manchu Qinq dynasty, ending four thousand years of dynastic rule. Republic inaugurated.

1912–28 First period of Republic with capital at Peking. Power in hands of military commanders ('warlords'). Sun Yat-sen's Nationalist Party (Kuomintang, Guomindang) resists Peking warlords.

1919 May 4 Demonstrations in Peking against betrayal of China at Paris Peace Conference lead to national movement protest.

1924–27 Revolutionary alliance between Nationalist Party and small Communist Party (founded 1921) against northern warlords weakens after death of Sun Yat-sen (1925) and ends in civil war when Sun's successor Chiang Kai-shek turns on Communists in April 1927.

1931–37 Japan seizes North-east China (Manchuria), creates puppet state of Manchukuo (1932) with Pu Yi as emperor (1934), continues aggression in China.

1934–35 Main forces of Red Army break out of Nationalist encirclement in south China and after year-long trek across harsh terrain end up in Shaanxi province in north-west (Long March).

1936 Yan'an (Yenan) in Shaanxi becomes Communist head-quarters.

1937 July Outbreak of fighting between Chinese and Japanese forces at Lugouqiao (Marco Polo Bridge) outside Peking develops into full-scale Japanese invasion of China.

Aug Red Army troops in north China redesignated Eighth Route Army of National Revolutionary Army as Communists join Nationalists in united front against Japan.

Aug–Dec Chiang Kai-shek throws main Nationalist forces into battle for Shanghai and is defeated with heavy losses. Fall of Nanjing (13 December) and Hangzhou (23 December).

1938 March–Apr Chinese victory at Battle of Taierzhuang only slows Japanese advance.

Oct Fall of Wuhan to Japanese.

1938–45 During rest of Japanese war relations between Nationalists and Communists deteriorate. Nationalists grow weaker while Communists grow stronger.

1945 Aug Japanese surrender opens way for new conflicts between Nationalists and Communists despite US attempts at mediation.

1946 July New civil war begins. Although heavily outnumbered, Communists slowly win ascendancy.

1948 Dec Communist forces besiege Peking.

1949 Jan 31 Communists enter Peking.

Apr Communist armies cross Yangtse, taking Nationalist capital Nanjing (23 April) and Shanghai (27 May).

Oct 1 Mao proclaims the establishment of the People's Republic of China in its new capital, Peking.

1950 June Outbreak of Korean War.

Nov Chinese 'volunteers' drive US forces back from Yalu river.

1950–53 Land redistribution in villages. Political campaigns begin.

1953 Ceasefire in Korea.

1953–57 First five-year plan for industrialization of China.

1955–56 Socialization of agriculture, industry and commerce.

1956–57 Limited free speech of 'Hundred Flowers' period ends in repression and 'Anti-Rightist' campaign.

1958 Launch of ill-fated Great Leap Forward in attempt to pull China out of backwardness. People's communes created.

1960–62 Great Leap policies result in extensive famine costing at least 20 million lives.

1965 Dec Mao launches Cultural Revolution.

1966 Cultural Revolution gathers momentum. Red Guards appear.

1967–68 Cultural Revolution's most violent phase with many local civil wars. After summer 1968 Red Guards sent off to countryside.

1969 Heavily publicized border conflicts with Soviet Union.

1971 Visits of US table-tennis team ('ping-pong diplomacy') and Henry Kissinger to China pave way to rapprochement.

Sept Death of Mao's heir apparent Lin Biao.

Oct People's Republic takes China seat at United Nations.

1972 Feb US President Nixon visits China.

1972–74 Many senior officials overthrown in Cultural Revolution return to office, including Deng Xiaoping.

1976 Jan 8 Death of Zhou Enlai.

March–Apr Demonstrations in Tiananmen Square in Peking implicitly demand end to Maoist policies.

Apr Deng Xiaoping dismissed from all posts. Hua Guofeng made premier.

Sept 9 Death of Mao.

Oct Huo Guofeng and Peking garrison stage coup d'état, arresting four leading Maoist members of Political Bureau including Mao's widow Jiang Qing. Hua becomes chairman of Communist Party and launches his very own personality cult.

1977 Deng Xiaoping returns to positions of power. University entrance exams reintroduced.

1978 Dec Third Plenum of the 11th Central Committee of the Communist Party of China launches Deng's reform plans.

1979 One-child family campaign begins. Invasion of Vietnam.

1980–84 Dismantling of collective agriculture as land is contracted out to peasant households. Opening up of China to foreign capital. Establishment of Special Economic Zones. With raising of procurement prices for agricultural products China risks inflation-led growth.

1983 Campaign against 'spiritual pollution' of foreign influence ends in fiasco.

1984 Campaign against crime leads to many more offences being made capital ones. Thousands of executions each year thereafter, and countless young people exiled to North-west.

1985 Britain agrees to surrender Hong Kong in 1997.

1986 Dec Student demonstrations in many cities demanding faster reform.

1987 Jan Hu Yaobang blamed for student troubles and dismissed as general secretary of Communist Party. Campaign against 'bourgeois liberalization' launched that fizzles out later in the year.

The Photographers

Frontispiece: René Burri 1965
1. René Burri 1985
2. Walter Bosshard 1938
3. Bruno Barbey
4. Marc Riboud 1965
5. Marc Riboud 1965
6. René Burri 1964
7. René Burri 1965
8. René Burri 1964
9. Marc Riboud 1957
10. Marc Riboud 1965
11. Marc Riboud 1965
12. René Burri 1964
13. Marc Riboud
14. Hiroshi Hamaya 1956
15. Hiroshi Hamaya 1956
16. Henri Cartier-Bresson 1958
17. Marc Riboud 1957
18. Thomas Hopker 1985
19. Helen Snow 1938
20. Robert Capa 1938
21. Robert Capa 1938
22. Helen Snow 1938
23. Helen Snow 1938
24. Walter Bosshard 1939
25. Robert Capa 1938
26. Robert Capa 1938
27. Robert Capa 1938
28. Walter Bosshard 1938
29. Walter Bosshard 1938
30. Walter Bosshard 1938
31-34. Robert Capa 1938
35. Robert Capa 1938
36. Robert Capa 1938
37. Robert Capa 1938
38. Robert Capa 1938
39. Henri Cartier-Bresson 1948
40. Helen Snow 1937

41. Henri Cartier-Bresson 1949
42. Henri Cartier-Bresson 1949
43. Henri Cartier-Bresson 1949
44. Henri Cartier-Bresson 1949
45. Henri Cartier-Bresson 1949
46. Henri Cartier-Bresson 1949
47. Henri Cartier-Bresson 1949
48. Marc Riboud 1957
49. Henri Cartier-Bresson 1958
50. Marc Riboud 1957
51. Hiroshi Hamaya 1956
52. Hiroshi Hamaya 1956
53. Marc Riboud 1957
54. Marc Riboud 1957
55. Henri Cartier-Bresson 1958
56. Henri Cartier-Bresson 1958
57. René Burri 1964
58. René Burri 1964
59. René Burri 1964
60. René Burri 1964
61. Marc Riboud 1965
62. René Burri 1964
63. Marc Riboud 1965
64. Marc Riboud 1965
65. Marc Riboud 1965
66. Marc Riboud 1957
67. Marc Riboud 1957
68. Marc Riboud 1965
69. René Burri 1964
70. Marc Riboud 1965
71. Marc Riboud 1965
72. Marc Riboud 1957
73. Marc Riboud 1957
74. Marc Riboud 1965
75. René Burri 1965
76. René Burri 1965
77. Bruno Barbey 1980
78. Marc Riboud 1965

79. René Burri 1964
80. René Burri 1964
81. René Burri 1964
82. René Burri 1964
83. René Burri 1964
84. Marc Riboud 1965
85. Marc Riboud 1971
86. Marc Riboud 1957
87. René Burri 1965
88. René Burri 1965
89. René Burri 1964
90. René Burri 1964
91. Marc Riboud 1965
92. Bruno Barbey 1973
93. Bruno Barbey 1973
94. Bruno Barbey 1973
95. Marc Riboud 1965
96. René Burri 1964
97. Hiroshi Hamaya 1956
98. Marc Riboud 1971
99. Marc Riboud 1965
100. Marc Riboud 1965
101. Inge Morath 1978
102. Marc Riboud 1957
103. Costas Manos 1979
104. René Burri 1964
105. Bruno Barbey 1973
106. Marc Riboud 1971
107. Marc Riboud 1965
108. Elliott Erwitt 1978
109. René Burri 1964
110. René Burri 1964
111. Martine Franck 1980
112. Marc Riboud 1971
113. Elliott Erwitt 1978
114. Inge Morath 1978
115. Martine Franck 1980
116. Inge Morath 1979

117. Raymond Depardon 1986
118. Thomas Hopker 1985
119. Thomas Hopker 1985
120. Elliott Erwitt 1978
121. Inge Morath 1978
122. Inge Morath 1978
123. Eve Arnold 1984
124. Martine Franck 1980
125. Martine Franck 1980
126. Martine Franck 1980
127. Patrick Zachmann 1982
128. Raymond Depardon 1985
129. Thomas Hopker 1985
130. Hiroji Kubota 1985
131. Guy Le Querec 1984
132. Marc Riboud 1979
133. Guy Le Querec 1984
134. Eve Arnold 1984
135. Bruno Barbey 1985
136. Bruno Barbey 1985
137. Eve Arnold 1984
138. René Burri 1986
139. Inge Morath 1978
140. Inge Morath 1978
141. Guy Le Querec 1984
142. Guy Le Querec 1984
143. Inge Morath 1979
144. Guy Le Querec 1984
145. Patrick Zachmann 1982
146. Martine Franck 1980
147. Inge Morath 1978
148. Guy Le Querec 1984
149. Guy Le Querec 1984
150. Martine Franck 1980
151. Elliott Erwitt 1978
152. Bruno Barbey 1985
153. René Burri 1985